Palliative Perspective

Robyn Louise

BookLeaf Publishing

Presentation by *BookLeaf Publishing*

Web: www.bookleafpub.com

E-mail: info@bookleafpub.com

ISBN: 9789357210164

First edition 2022

DEDICATION

Special dedication to my truly wonderful best friend Catherine Turner.

See you later Alligator xx

Do the Angels play?

"A vision of heaven
Appeared to me today.
And dear i was so glad
To learn the angels play!

My mother and father
And Brothers were there too,
But don't worry dear
I'll save a place for you".

Time passed by
As i watched her fade away.
No more scrabble games
Did we ever play.

As her time approached
I held her hand and cried.
She simply looked at me,
Kissed my hand and smiled.

"Do the angles play?" i ask
As we say our goodbyes.
She whispers "Yes of course my dear"
And closes her eyes.

Bingo

We don't just like Bingo,
Don't you know?
We like board games and pub games
And planting things to grow.

We don't just like a cup of tea,
Can't you see?
We like cans of pop, hot chocolate
And a tipple of sherry.

We don't just like wartime tunes,
Didn't you hear?
We like rock and roll, country
And classical my dear.

So next time you reach for the bingo
Once more;
Perhaps you'll stop, acknowledge us
And Pause.

We are individual people,
Not all the same.
Let's start a conversation like,
'Hello, What's your name?'

Seasons

"Of all the seasons of the year,
I like Autumn best.
Summertime has gone i fear
but lingers in the West.

People still swim and enjoy the sun.
Off of work at weekends,
Enjoying the harvest fun
With family and friends.

Farmers are busy with their lands,
Hay is neatly stacked.
Housewives are bust with their jams
And larder shelves are packed.

There's local produce in the shops
And on the market stall.
People have all had good crops
And there's enough for all.

These are the reasons
why i like it so.
She's the queen of seasons
between the sun and snow."

She smiles so intently,
Her clouded eyes are bright.
Reminiscing meant she
Wondered in delight.

Cathy's Poem

I Know a carer called Kate,
Who thinks she's my best mate.
She helps me wash and dress,
And I must confess…
The job she does is first rate.

I know a carer called Carol,
Who one day fell into a barrel,
But she was found
Before she drowned,
And quickly put on dry apparel.

I know a carer called Kelly,
Who was rather fond of fruit jelly.
She'd put away,
A lot every day.
Sometimes when watching the telly.

I know a carer called Christine,
But she's commonly known as Chris.
Her appearance is perfectly pristine
And she likes to be known by this.

Deborah is another carer,
But she's not known by this name.

People will call her
And say that she's cheeky,
She goes along with the game.

We have a carer called Sue,
Who knows a good thing or two.
She's wise past her years
In the ways of our care,
And a very good job she will do.

We have a carer called Gina,
And nobody could be more keener.
She will bring you food
To eat which is good.
You'll like her as soon as you've seen her

We have a carer called Kervin,
His aptness is really unnerving.
As he covers the ground
Running around,
Our thanks he is deserving.

Kathy is another young girl,
Who puts all the staff in a whirl.
She gets in a state
Putting things straight,
And her hair has no trace of a curl.

There is a girl called Katrina,

Who's on par with friend Gina.
They go around together
In all sorts of weather.
You would know who she is if you see her.

There is a carer called Pauline,
Who never did anything mean.
In every way
To all she would say.
To go out with you I am keen.

I have a carer called Hayley,
Who sees me once or twice daily.
She brings me food
Sometimes when she's good,
And if asked will sing with me gayly.

I have a carer called Robyn,
And she had a fine mare called Dobbin.
She's a fine horse indeed
Takes her where she will need.
And on her saddle, she goes bobbin.

I am sure there will be many more,
But I can't recall the names of them all
But they are not forgotten.

Love at this time, Catherine x

Cathy's Happy Harvest Memories

There is a time in October
Known as the Harvest festival.
The years work had been done,
And now it is time for fun!

The crops have all been gathered
And safely stored away.
Now the time has come
To have a holiday.

The big barn has been swept,
Tables all set out.
We are all looking forward to some fun.
Of that there is no doubt.

The Children all have gathered
And homework has been done.
From the age of seven,
They look forward to some fun.

From the oldest to the youngest,
They are all dressed in their best.
The young folk are courting,
Put true love to the test.

The Vicar has come in
And cooperation too…
They are looking forward,
To all the fun things to do.

The town band has gathered,
And struck a merry tune.
They are the songs of yesteryear.
Oh, what a tune!

The apples are strung on strings,
Everyone tries to catch one
As it gently swings.
Other games they like to play
With spiced buns to eat.

The MC is in charge
Keeping order there;
With tea and coffee to drink
And even home brewed beer!

All the Children will have squash,
With jellies and trifles to eat.
Soon children will go home
Whilst adults stay on, meet and greet.

Dancing will soon begin,
And those who are able

Will sure want to join in.
As the evening progresses,
The stars come out to shine.
Everyone says they've had such a lovely time.

Many thanks are spoken,
All is packed away.
They'll do the same next year
On this special day.

"You're Just A Carer"

"You're just a carer".
An 'unskilled' profession.
Yet to our patients
We make a lasting impression.

"You just wipe bottoms".
An 'undignified' task.
Yet there's much more to skin integrity
Than you care to ask.

"You just make tea".
An 'insignificant' thing.
Yet nutrition and fluids are key
so cups of tea we shall bring.

"You just sit holding her hand
Whilst others work hard to make a living".
Yet we wipe away tears
And listen to their fears
In place of friends who are missing.

"You are just a carer".
An 'unskilled' profession.
Yet to our patients
We are much more, no question.

Wander

Though I may wander,
I needn't be alone.
Take my hand and wander too,
Until I'm safely home.

Though I may not remember,
Please know I still feel
Such love and warmth around you.
That, I know, is real.

Though I may lose my temper,
Try not to shout.
There's so much I wish to express,
I just can't get it out.

Though some days I am distant,
Come and be with me here.
Your presence is all I need
To help ease this awful fear.

Though I may live in memories gone by,
Please don't drag me into present times.
Reminisce with yours truly,
Reassure my mind.

Though I may wander,
I needn't be alone.
Take my hand and wander too,
Until I'm safely home.

Like Flowers

Like seedlings,
We start off small.
Not yet knowing
What the world has in store.

Like buds,
We grow a little more each day.
The seasons of life
Help guide us on our way.

Like flowers,
We bloom into full beauty.
Showing the world
Just how we fulfil our duty.

But just like flowers,
We mature.
Ageing each day
And wilting all the more.

Time Past

I wave at you and smile,
I try to say hello.
But you are always busy,
Rushing to and fro.

I ask for your company,
Perhaps you'll sit a while?
But your reply remains the same,
'I simply don't have time'.

My darling, time is precious
And lessens every day.
So could you spare a minute,
Please don't turn away.

I'm afraid, you see
Because my time is running fast.
It's lonely and scary
And I'm quickly becoming past.

So dear spare a moment
As my time is running out too.
And I'd long for nothing more
Than to spend my time with you.

How I wish

Blank stares,
Forgotten names.
How I wish recognition
Would grace your face.

Emotional outbursts,
Confused states.
How I wish there was something
That could ease your pain.

Muddled words,
Slow in pace.
How I wish communication
Hadn't been erased.

Lucid dreams,
Delusional ways.
How I wish Dementia
Could be cured today.

Learn from my mistakes

Time and time again,
I was told "It's not your fault".
But I stayed,
When I should of walked.
I pretended I was fine,
When I was not.
I let myself
Be used and blamed,
So now I'm left
Feeling so ashamed.
Darling please,
Learn from my mistakes.
If you don't feel safe,
Then walk away.
As now I don't believe
that "It's not my fault"
Because I stayed silent,
When I should of talked.

Anyone who tells you

Anyone who tells you
Care is glamorous ,is lying.
We deal with bodily fluids,
vomiting, and even 'Poonamis!'.

Anyone who tells you
Care is easy, is misleading.
It's twelve hour shifts, nights and days,
Not overly appealing.

Anyone who tells you
Care is unskilled, is dishonest.
The task of Counsellor, Chef, Cleaner, Carer
And friend is upon us.

Anyone who tells you
Care is well paid, is naïve.
But let me tell you caring
Is the biggest honour to receive.

Beautifully Strange

It's beautifully strange this feeling,
Whenever he is near.
And though I am cautious,
I'm not trembling with fear.

It's beautifully strange this feeling,
Difficult to explain.
When he pulls me closer,
I don't feel scared but safe.

It's beautifully strange this feeling,
Trying to adjust.
Knowing we can be ourselves
And to be myself is enough.

It's beautifully strange this feeling,
Seeing him smile.
All other stress and worry
Just goes for a while.

This beautifully strange feeling
That happens when close to you,
Brings me hope and happiness
For a wonderful anew.

Liquorice Toffee

"Please could you bring me
Some Liquorice toffee"
She would say, smiling with glee.
Of course I'd oblige
And reach to my side
To obtain the favoured sweets.

Now I walk past the sweet variety
In shops, and smile in memory.
I remember the times
With you in our lives,
Eating your Liquorice toffee.

Ocean of Grief

Emotions change just like the tide
One wave of happy
One wave of sad and
One wave of calm to soothe the mind.

Grief stands strong as the waves unfold
Calm on the surface
But whats underneath
Nobody knows the strength that it holds.

Bereavement is unpredictable, as is the sea.
Just when it's still
And you feel able to swim
You are pulled back under to the depths within
thee.

Breathe

Noise...
Overbearing, undistinguishable noise closing in from every angle. The unmissable sound of thudding, beating louder and louder until you feel a pounding from within your ribcage.

Brightness...
Overwhelming brightness enclosing you, eyes screwed shut, desperately trying to gain some relief. Teardrops threatening to cascade as you continue to fight and hold them back.

Fear...
Wave after wave of irrational fear, paralysed from panic. Your breath quickening, muscles tensing and body trembling, yet still you can't breathe, still you can't breathe.

Time...
It ticks on whilst your frozen with fear, every second filling an eternity.
This will pass, this WILL pass.
Slowly your body relaxes, the light becomes bearable and you can hear once more.

Breathe...
Inhale,
Exhale.
Feel the ground beneath you as you come back to reality.
It has passed, you are safe...

When I say

When I say 'You don't know how wonderful you are',
Just know that it is true.
When I'm sad or teary,
You care for me too.
It is strange to me, this kindness
That you show each day, anew.
But it's more than that you see,
These words are so subdued
For trying to express how beautiful you are,
From my point of view.
Passionate & Caring, Patient & Kind.
To name just a few
And when I think of these words combined
Well, they lead me straight to you.

In loving memory

I was new to the care world
When I first met you.
It never crossed my mind
That we would share a friendship too.

In our evening hour
Scrabble we would play.
I never really expected
To lose every single day

Maybe the angels are better
At scrabble though I tried,
It took you no time at all
To triple my score in size.

I looked forward to a childhood story
Or even a little song.
Somewhere over the rainbow
Or your favourite, Flanders and Swan.

I listened to accounts of your children
And how proud of them you are.
I know how much you loved them,
easured joys by far.

Today we celebrate you in our memories
Of which we shall not part.
God may have you in his keeping,
We have you in our hearts.

These special memories of you
Will always bring a smile.
So, see you later Alligator,
In a while crocodile.

www.ingramcontent.com/pod-product-compliance
Lightning Source LLC
Chambersburg PA
CBHW062205160726
48282CB00027B/1009
* 9 7 8 9 3 5 7 2 1 0 1 6 4 *